Contents

Phonemes

Ready read this

All words are made up of sounds. These sounds are called phonemes.

A phoneme may be made up of one or more letters.

b + oy = boy

This word is made up of two phonemes.

g + ir + l = girl

This word is made up of three phonemes.

Steady practise this

1 Put together the jigsaw pieces. Say the sounds out loud and write down the word.

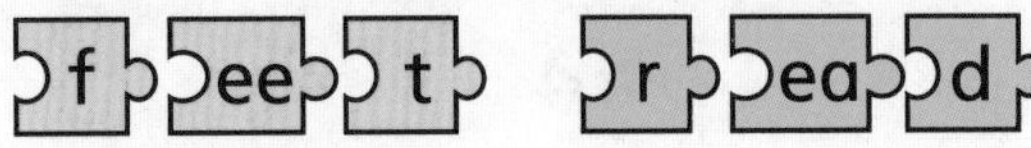

f ee t	r ea d	t ea ch	sh ee p
feet ______	________	________	________
r ai n	t r ay	j ai l	d ay
________	________	________	________
b oa t	sh ow	s l ow	c oa ch
________	________	________	________

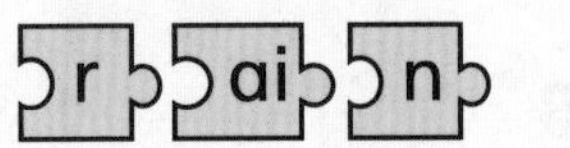

2 Complete the missing phoneme.

ee **ea**

s________

ee **ea**

b________

ai **ay**

n_____l

ai **ay**

p________

oa **ow**

g_____t

oa **ow**

m________

ANSWERS: (1) feet, read, teach, sheep, rain, tray, jail, day, boat, show, slow, coach; (2) sea, bee, nail, pay, goat, mow

Go test yourself

Choose the correct phoneme to complete each word.

1	b___d	(er/ir)	
2	enj___	(oi/oy)	
3	f___nd	(ou/ow)	
4	br___d	(e/ea)	
5	b___l	(oi/oy)	
6	tr___	(igh/y)	
7	sp___t	(or/aw)	
8	st___	(ur/ar)	
9	bl___	(oo/ue)	
10	n___	(ou/ow)	

Write the word here.

Colour a star for each answer you get right.

Zoom your challenge

Write as many words as possible that contain the following phonemes:

oo	ur	ar	igh	ea

ANSWERS: (1) bird; (2) enjoy; (3) found; (4) bread; (5) boil; (6) try; (7) sport; (8) star; (9) blue; (10) now

Verbs

Ready read this

A verb is a doing word. It tells us about an action of some sort.

Today I **am playing** football.

This is happening now. We say the verb is in the present tense.

Yesterday I **played** cricket.

This happened in the past. We say the verb is in the past tense.

Steady practise this

1 Fill in the missing verbs. The verbs are all in the present tense.

a I am ______ (paint) a picture.

b The sun is ______ (shine).

c The lady is ______ (carry) a basket.

d The children are ______ (ride) their bikes.

e A frog is ______ (hop) along.

2 Choose the correct verb for each sentence. The verbs are all in the past tense.

bought popped broke hurried snored

a The old man ______ in his sleep.

b I ______ some new trainers on Saturday.

c The naughty girl ______ all the balloons.

ANSWERS: 1 (a) painting; (b) shining; (c) carrying; (d) riding; (e) hopping
2 (a) snored; (b) bought; (c) popped

Verbs

Go test yourself

Fill in the correct verbs.

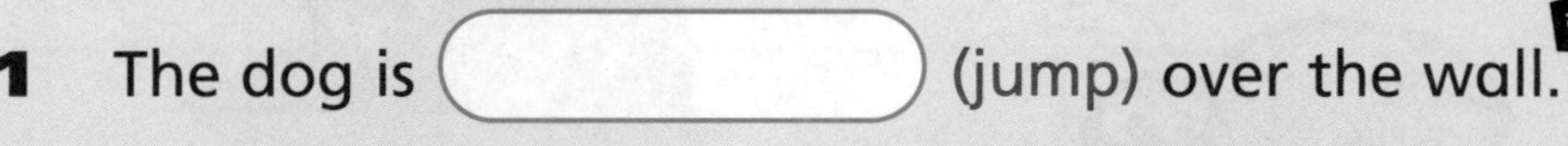

1 The dog is ______ (jump) over the wall.

2 Last week I ______ (act) in a play.

3 Whem Tom threw the ball, Sam ______ (catch) it.

4 Anna ______ (brush) her hair before she went out.

5 Mrs Smith is ______ (dig) her garden.

6 Yesterday I ______ (climb) a tall tree.

7 When I got home, I ______ (try) to do my homework.

8 The children are ______ (make) a model.

9 My friends are ______ (smile) at me.

10 As we went by, we all ______ (see) the accident.

Colour a star ★ for each answer you get right.

1 Write five sentences about things you did yesterday. Underline the verbs in your sentences.

2 Look out the window. Write five sentences about things you can see happening right now. Underline the verbs in the sentences.

ANSWERS: (1) jumping; (2) acted; (3) caught; (4) brushed; (5) digging; (6) climbed; (7) tried; (8) making; (9) smiling; (10) saw

Spelling strategies

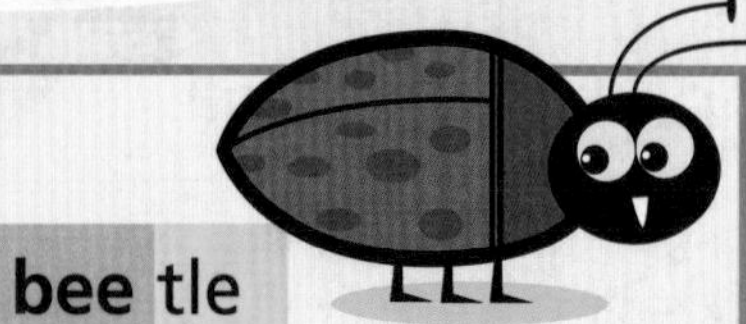

bee tle

We can often find smaller words 'hiding' inside longer words.

hedge + hog = hedgehog

Sometimes a word is made up of two shorter words joined together.

Steady
practise this

1 Make some words.

ape

c ape	t_____	sh_____	gr_____	esc_____
cape	______	______	______	______

ant

p____	w____	ch____	inf____	eleph____
______	______	______	______	______

2 Find and underline a smaller word 'hiding' inside each animal, bird or insect.

<u>bad</u>ger, bear, budgerigar, camel, caterpillar, chimpanzee, gorilla, hamster, kitten, monkey, octopus, orangutan, ostrich, panther

ANSWERS: (1) cape, tape, shape, grape, escape, pant, want, chant, infant, elephant; (2) **some possible answers**: bad; ear; budge; came; cat; pill; him; pan; go; ill; ham; kit, ten; key; top, us; ran, tan; rich; pan, ant, her

Spelling strategies

Go test yourself

Match the words on ribbon A with those on ribbon B to make the name of an animal, insect, bird or sea creature.

Write the names here.

	A	B	
1	bull	wig	
2	butter	bird	
3	ear	dog	bulldog
4	gold	fly	
5	lady	fish	
6	rein	deer	
7	pea	hog	
8	grey	cock	
9	hedge	eater	
10	ant	hound	

Colour a star for each answer you get right.

Zoom your challenge

Think of as many words as you can beginning with the words below.

The first one has been done for you.

snow:	snowball snowman snowflake snowfall
foot:	
rain:	
some:	
head:	

ANSWERS: (1) bulldog; (2) butterfly; (3) earwig; (4) goldfish; (5) ladybird; (6) reindeer; (7) peacock; (8) greyhoun
(9) hedgehog; (10) anteater

Nouns

Ready
read this

A noun is a naming word.

A noun may be the name of a person, place or thing.

A sailor is on a boat in the harbour.

a person | a thing | a place

1 Underline the name of the person in each sentence.

a A pilot flies aeroplanes.

b A florist sells flowers.

c A plumber fits and repairs water pipes.

d A dentist looks after our teeth.

2 Fill in the missing place.

Use these words
museum garage
bank

a A ______ is where people keep money.

b A ______ is where cars are kept.

c A ______ is where old and interesting things are kept.

3 Fill in the names of the things that you think are being described.

a ______ You use this for telling the time.

b ______ This is a musical instrument with black and white keys.

c ______ This is a tool used for cutting wood.

ANSWERS: 1 (a) pilot; (b) florist; (c) plumber; (d) dentist; 2 (a) bank; (b) garage; (c) museum; 3 (a) clock; (b) piano; (c) saw

Go test yourself

Look at each noun below. Is it the name of a person, place or thing?

		Person	Place	Thing
1	clown			
2	chair			
3	library			
4	cinema			
5	doctor			
6	bucket			
7	supermarket			
8	fork			
9	teacher			
10	detective			

Put a tick in the correct flower.

Colour a star ★ for each answer you get right.

Find twenty nouns in a book. Write down if they are the name of a person, place or thing.

ANSWERS: (1) person; (2) thing; (3) place; (4) place; (5) person; (6) thing; (7) place; (8) thing; (9) person; (10) perso

Alphabetical order

It is important to understand alphabetical order.

Many books (e.g. dictionaries) are arranged in alphabetical order.

apple	banana	coconut	peach	pineapple	plum

The names of these fruits are arranged in alphabetical order according to the first letter.

The names of these fruits are arranged in alphabetical order according to the second letter.

Steady practise this

1 Write the words in alphabetical order.

I've done the first one!

a car, ambulance, boat

ambulance — boat — car

b submarine, train, rocket

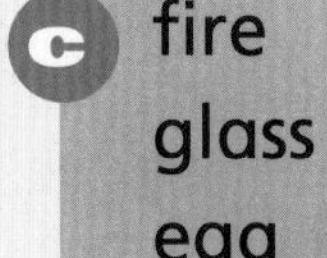

c fire, glass, egg, hammer

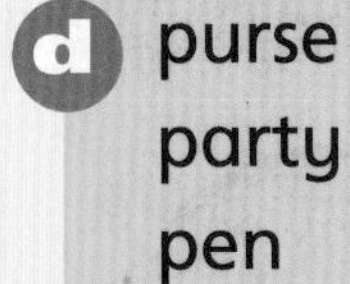

d purse, party, pen

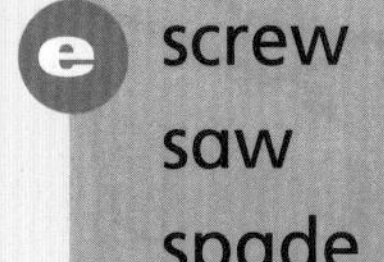

e screw, saw, spade

ANSWERS: (b) rocket, submarine, train; (c) egg, fire, glass, hammer; (d) party, pen, purse; (e) saw, screw, spade

Alphabetical order

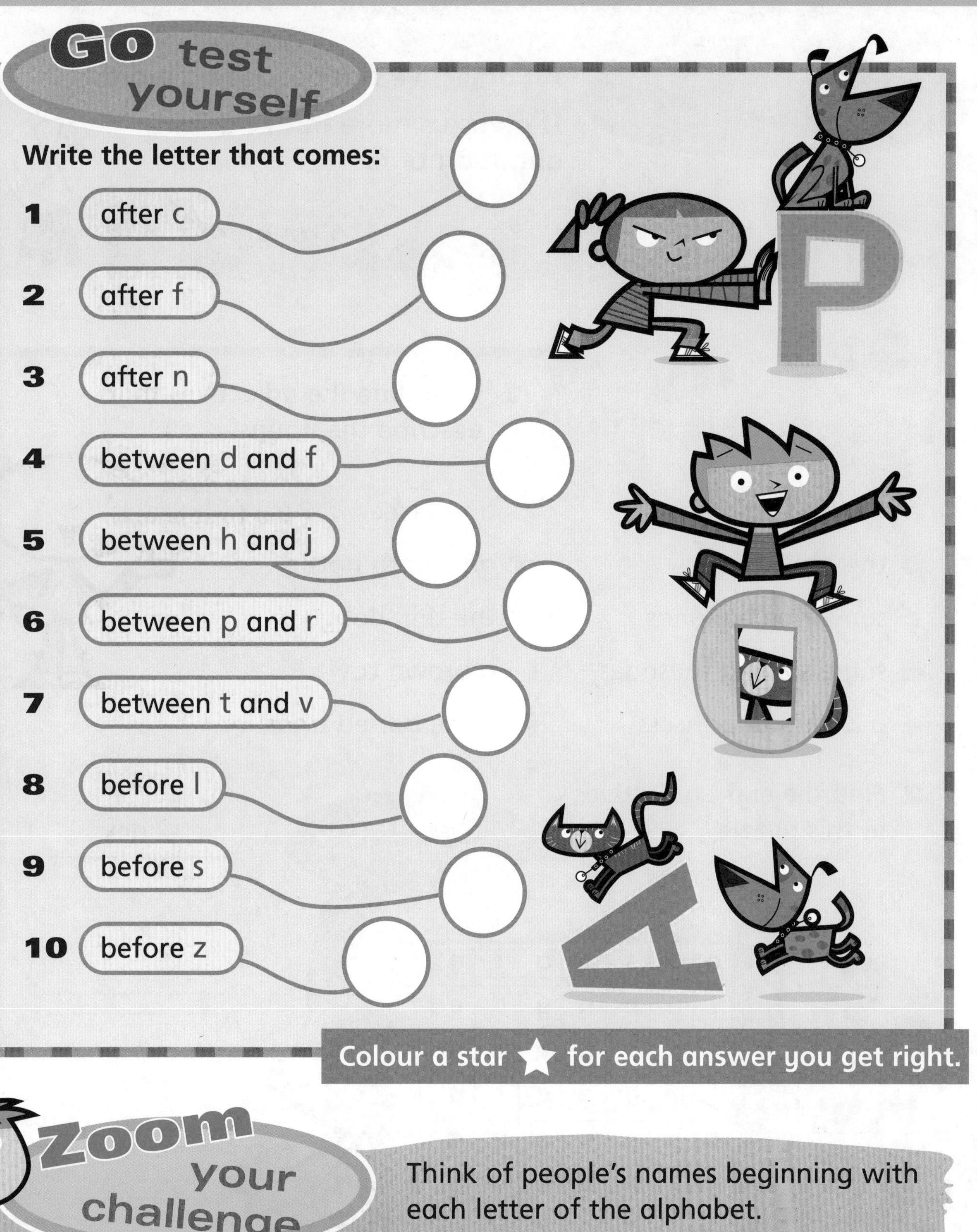

Go test yourself

Write the letter that comes:

1 after c

2 after f

3 after n

4 between d and f

5 between h and j

6 between p and r

7 between t and v

8 before l

9 before s

10 before z

Colour a star for each answer you get right.

Zoom your challenge

Think of people's names beginning with each letter of the alphabet.

Write the names in alphabetical order.

ANSWERS: (1) d; (2) g; (3) o; (4) e; (5) i; (6) q; (7) u; (8) k; (9) r; (10) y

2 3 4 5 6 7 8 9 10

Adjectives

An adjective is a describing word.

It gives us more information about a noun.

a <u>rough</u> sea

Steady practise this

1 Underline the adjectives that describe the nouns.

I've done the first one!

- **a** a <u>bitter</u> lemon
- **b** the old lady
- **c** some ripe bananas
- **d** some sizzling sausages
- **e** a beautiful princess
- **f** a tall tree
- **g** an empty bottle
- **h** the tiny baby
- **i** a brown cow
- **j** some buried treasure

2 Find the eight adjectives in this puzzle.

Write the adjectives here.

a	b	s	c	a	r	y	c
f	u	n	n	y	d	e	f
g	h	i	h	e	a	v	y
j	m	o	d	e	r	n	k
o	p	e	n	o	p	q	r
s	t	w	d	e	e	p	x
w	i	d	e	z	y	v	s
b	n	s	m	o	o	t	h

scary

______

______

______

______

______

______

______

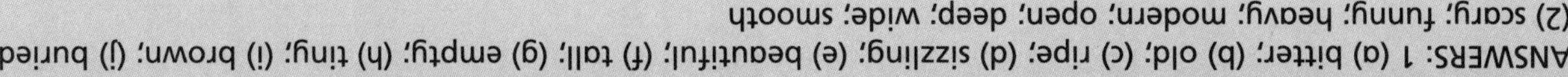
ANSWERS: 1 (a) bitter; (b) old; (c) ripe; (d) sizzling; (e) beautiful; (f) tall; (g) empty; (h) tiny; (i) brown; (j) buried
(2) scary; funny; heavy; modern; open; deep; wide; smooth

Go test yourself

Choose the most suitable adjective to complete each phrase.

1 A ________ (heavy, bright) weight

2 An ________ (ugly, interesting) book

3 The ________ (funny, fair) clown

4 Some ________ (green, black) clouds

5 An ________ (amusing, old) castle

6 Some ________ (quiet, dirty) marks

7 A ________ (loud, bold) noise

8 A ________ (beautiful, handsome) prince

9 The ________ (sharp, brave) soldier

10 Some ________ (empty, excited) bottles

Colour a star ★ for each answer you get right.

Work out these adjectives – all the vowels have been left out.

gntl	strng	qut	plyfl	bg	scrd

hrrbl	frghtnd	xpnsv	plsnt	smll	cnnng

ANSWERS: (1) heavy; (2) interesting; (3) funny; (4) black; (5) old; (6) dirty; (7) loud; (8) handsome; (9) brave; (10)

Punctuation marks

Ready
read this

Punctuation marks make our writing easier to read and understand.

This is my car.

Most sentences end with a full stop.

Do you like my car?

Questions end with a question mark.

What a lovely car!

Exclamation marks show that we feel strongly about something.

Steady
practise this

1 Match up the questions and answers. Put in the missing full stops or question marks.

a	What is that noise __	It is green __
b	Where are you going __	It is our next-door neighbour __
c	What colour is grass __	It is the sound of thunder __
d	Who is at the door __	It is after February __
e	When is March __	I'm going home __

2 Decide if these sentences are questions or exclamations. Put in the missing punctuation marks.

a	Do you like sport __	f	This apple pie is wonderful __
b	Please stop shouting __	g	Who is winning __
c	Are you afraid of spiders __	h	I hate snakes __
d	Get out of here quickly __	i	Look out __
e	You're great __	j	Where are my slippers __

ANSWERS: 1 (b) I'm going home. (c) It is green. (d) It is our next-door neighbour. (e) It is after February.
2 (a) ? (b) ! (c) ? (d) ! (e) ! (f) ! (g) ? (h) ! (i) ! (j) ?

Punctuation marks

Go test yourself

Put in the missing full stops, question marks and exclamation marks.

1. How are you today __
2. Come here at once __
3. The farmer milked the cows __
4. What is the time __
5. It's not fair __
6. The clouds were black __
7. Who is the Prime Minister __
8. Bees live in a hive __
9. When may we go __
10. Don't do that __

Colour a star for each answer you get right.

Zoom your challenge

Which punctuation mark do you think is used the most? Investigate to find out.

★ Choose any page of a storybook.

★ Count how many full stops, question marks and exclamation marks you can see.

ANSWERS: (1) ? (2) ! (3) . (4) ? (5) ! (6) . (7) ? (8) . (9) ? (10) !

10

Prefixes

A prefix is a group of letters that goes in front of a word.

A prefix often changes the meaning of a word.

happy

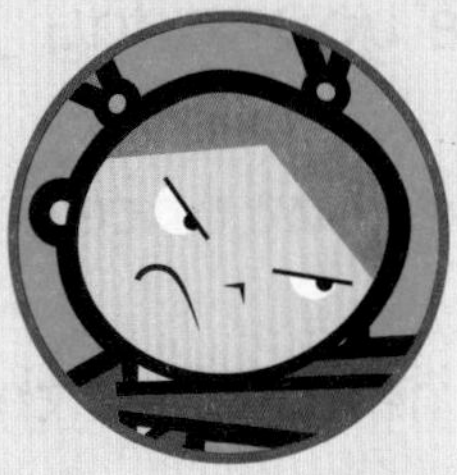

un + happy = unhappy

Steady
practise this

1 Add the prefix to make words.

un		
	pack	unpack
	well	
	do	
	cover	
	fair	

dis		
	appear	
	agree	
	trust	
	honest	
	obey	

2 Add the correct prefix to make each word mean the opposite.

a ____ cover b ____ agree c ____ honest

d ____ well e ____ fair f ____ appear

g ____ pack h ____ obey i ____ do

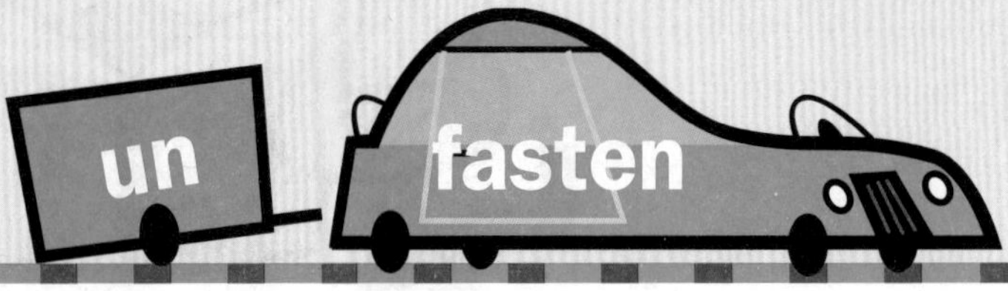

un fasten

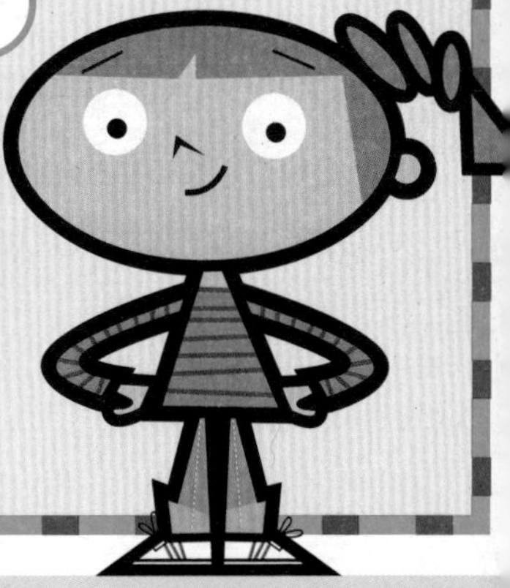

ANSWERS: (1) unpack, unwell, undo, uncover, unfair, disappear, disagree, distrust, dishonest, disobey
2 (a) uncover; (b) disagree; (c) dishonest; (d) unwell; (e) unfair; (f) disappear; (g) unpack; (h) disobey; (i) undo

Go test yourself

Choose the correct prefix to make a sensible word.

1 ____ able (un/mis)

2 ____ like (re/dis)

3 ____ correct (un/in)

4 ____ lead (dis/mis)

5 ____ grow (un/out)

6 ____ fix (dis/pre)

7 ____ place (mis/ex)

8 ____ fill (re/dis)

9 ____ behave (dis/mis)

10 ____ pack (dis/un)

Colour a star ★ for each answer you get right.

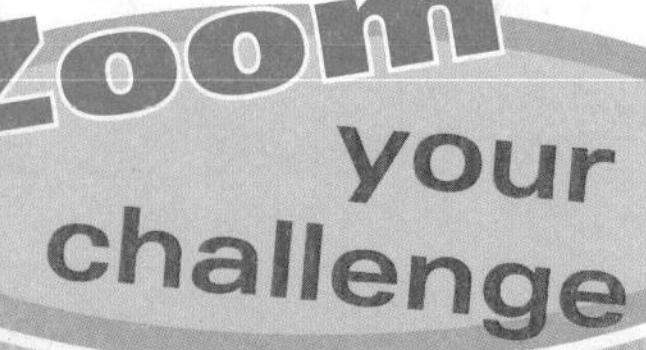

Zoom your challenge

Use a dictionary to find five words beginning with 're' and 'mis'.

re (meaning 'to do again', as in refill)

mis (meaning 'wrongly' or 'badly', as in misbehave)

ANSWERS: (1) unable; (2) dislike; (3) incorrect; (4) mislead; (5) outgrow; (6) prefix; (7) misplace; (8) refill; (9) misbe (10) unpack

Singular and plural

We can write nouns in the **singular** or **plural**.

Singular means just one.

one pram

lots of prams

Sometimes we just add an s to make the plural.

Plural means more than one.

one baby

lots of babies

Sometimes we have to change the spelling to make the plural.

Steady practise this

Complete the charts.

Take special care with these spellings!

a

Singular	Plural
one toy	two toys
one pen	two
one car	two
one bird	two
one clock	two
one	two hens
one	two sweets
one	two pegs
one	two steps
one	two rugs

b

Singular	Plural
one lady	two
one brush	two
one fox	two
one glass	two
one potato	two
one	two shelves
one	two thieves
one	two matches
one	two lorries
one	two volcanoes

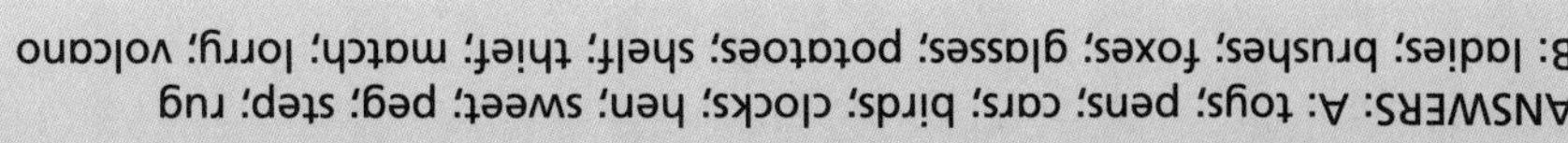

ANSWERS: A: toys; pens; cars; birds; clocks; hen; sweet; peg; step; rug
B: ladies; brushes; foxes; glasses; potatoes; shelf; thief; match; lorry; volcano

Singular and plural

Go test yourself

These plural nouns are all wrong! Rewrite each noun correctly.

1. Two babys
2. A few tomatos
3. A swarm of flys
4. Many knifes
5. Lots of churchs
6. Ten brushs
7. Five dishs
8. Lots of berrys
9. Two halfs
10. Three busses

Colour a star  for each answer you get right.

Zoom your challenge

A collective noun is a group or collection of things.

Think of a noun to complete these:

a bunch of		a box of		a library of	
a flock of		a herd of		a shoal of	
a fleet of		a pile of		a string of	

ANSWERS: (1) babies; (2) tomatoes; (3) flies; (4) knives; (5) churches; (6) brushes; (7) dishes; (8) berries; (9) halves; (10) buses

Common word endings

Look out for common letter patterns at the end of words.

One common word ending is le. a candle on a table

Steady practise this

1 Make some le words.

le

need____	hand____	ank____	gamb____	cand____	bug____
needle					

le

ang____	twink____	tumb____	tab____	sing____	spark____

2 Write the words that you made in the chart.

ble words	**dle** words	**gle** words	**kle** words

3 Choose cle or ple to complete each word.

uncle____	pur____	stee____	cir____	exam____
uncle				

cou____	sim____	arti____	mira____	cy____

ANSWERS: (1) needle, handle, ankle, gamble, candle, bugle, angle, twinkle, tumble, table, single, sparkle; (2) **ble:** gamble, tumble, table; **dle:** needle, handle,, candle; **gle:** bugle, angle, single; **kle:** ankle, twinkle, sparkle; (3) uncle; purple; steeple; circle; example; couple; simple; article; miracle; cycle

Common word endings

Go test yourself

Underline each le word.

Now write it here.

1	safjungleklw	jungle
2	zxcfeeblevbn	
3	qcradlewerty	
4	crackleptrdf	
5	mnbvcgrumble	
6	hgfbottleptr	
7	xzcvbapplemn	
8	qtablebvhfsh	
9	urbanglepltg	
10	zlittlewytrh	

Colour a star ★ for each answer you get right.

The endings al, el and il often sound the same as le. Find and write as many words as you can that end with:

al	el	il

ANSWERS: (1) jungle; (2) feeble; (3) cradle; (4) crackle; (5) grumble; (6) bottle; (7) apple; (8) table; (9) bangle; (10

Synonyms

Ready
read this

A **synonym** is a word with the same or **nearly the same** meaning as another word.

happy glad joyful cheerful

Steady
practise this

1 Complete each sentence with the verb that has the same meaning as the verb in brackets.

baked mended found cleaned bumped jumped

a I (discovered) ______ some money on the ground.

b I (cooked) ______ a cake.

c I (washed) ______ the car.

d I (leapt) ______ over the wall.

e I (banged) ______ my head.

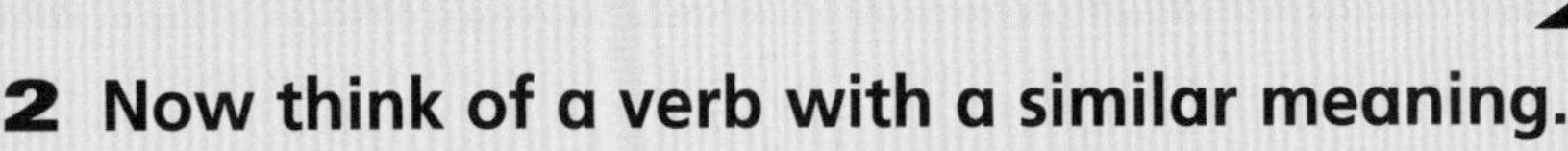

2 Now think of a verb with a similar meaning.

a I (tore) ______ my trousers.

b The man (dozed) ______ in the sun.

c The police officer (seized) ______ the thief.

d I (defeated) ______ my friend when we played tennis.

e The girl (shouted) ______ at the top of her voice.

ANSWERS: 1 (a) found; (b) baked; (c) cleaned; (d) jumped; (e) bumped
2 (a) ripped; (b) slept; (c) grabbed; (d) beat; (e) yelled

Synonyms

Match up the pairs of adjectives that have similar meanings.

1	big	scared
2	nasty	horrible
3	frightened	broad
4	wide	large
5	expensive	dear
6	small	tiny
7	sad	silly
8	easy	unhappy
9	foolish	fast
10	quick	simple

Colour a star for each answer you get right.

In place of each word below, write a synonym beginning with s.

begin		powerful		reveal	
quiet		cease		frighten	
odour		grasp		choose	

ANSWERS: (1) large; (2) horrible; (3) scared; (4) broad; (5) dear; (6) tiny; (7) unhappy; (8) simple; (9) silly; (10) fast

Silent letters

Ready
read this

Some words have silent letters, which we cannot hear. We do not pronounce these letters when we say the word.

knee

comb

palm

Sometimes they are at the beginning of a word.

Sometimes they are at the end of a word.

Sometimes they are within a word.

Steady
practise this

1 Each of these words contains a silent **k**, **b** or **l**.

Underline the silent letter in each word.

lamb	knot	comb	talk	know
palm	thumb	calf	knee	crumb
knit	climb	half	knife	calm

2 Now write each word in the chart below.

Words with a silent letter:		
at the beginning	at the end	inside

3 Write these words in the correct column of the chart:

folk **bomb** **knight** **chalk** **numb**
knob **yolk** **limb** **kneel**

ANSWERS: (2) **Beginning**: knot, know, knee, knit, knife; **End**: lamb, comb, thumb, crumb, climb; **Inside**: talk, palm, calf, half, calm (3) **Beginning**: knight, knob, kneel; **End**: bomb, numb, limb; **Inside**: folk, chalk, yolk

Silent letters

Go test yourself

Choose k, b or l to complete each word.

	Word		Whole word
1	limb__	→	limb
2	ha__f	→	
3	__nock	→	
4	__new	→	
5	ca__m	→	
6	clim__	→	
7	num__	→	
8	__nee	→	
9	com__	→	
10	yo__k	→	

Then write the whole word. I've done the first one!

See how many words you can find beginning with a silent w (e.g. 'write') and a silent g (e.g. 'gnome'). You can use your dictionary to help you.

ANSWERS: (1) limb, (2) half; (3) knock; (4) knew; (5) calm; (6) climb; (7) numb; (8) knee; (9) comb; (10) yolk

Speech marks

Ready
read this

In **pictures**, we write what a person says inside **speech bubbles**.

Jordan said,
'May I watch TV?'

In **writing**, we write the actual words inside **speech marks**.
The **first** word inside the speech marks always begins with a **capital letter**.

Steady
practise this

Write what you think each person said inside the correct set of speech marks.

I put the kettle on.

I've lost my sheep.

I was born on a Monday.

I fell off a wall.

I'm a merry old soul.

I can't eat any fat.

My cupboard is empty.

a Little Bo Peep said, '____________________'

b Humpty Dumpty said, '____________________'

c Jack Sprat said, '____________________'

d Polly said, '____________________'

e Old King Cole said, '____________________'

f Solomon Grundy said, '____________________'

g Old Mother Hubbard said, '____________________'

ANSWERS: (a) 'I've lost my sheep.' (b) 'I fell off the wall.' (c) 'I can't eat any fat.' (d) 'I put the kettle on.' (e) 'I'm a merry old soul.' (f) 'I was born on Monday.' (g) 'My cupboard is empty.'

Go test yourself

Add the missing speech marks.

1. The dentist said, Open wide, please.
2. Ali said, I would love a sweet.
3. Do you like my picture? the artist asked.
4. Let's go out, suggested Tom.
5. The jockey said, My job is riding horses.
6. The cow said, Moo.
7. Where is your book? the teacher asked.
8. It gets very hot in a bakery, the baker said.
9. I can't do it! Joanne exclaimed.
10. John screamed, Get away from me!

Colour a star ★ for each answer you get right.

Zoom your challenge

Practise using speech marks. Write a few things that these people might say:

- ★ an astronaut
- ★ a doctor
- ★ a hairdresser
- ★ a pop singer
- ★ a shop assistant
- ★ a chef

ANSWERS: (1) The dentist said, 'Open wide, please.' (2) Ali said, 'I would love a sweet.' (3) 'Do you like my picture?' the artist asked. (4) 'Let's go out,' suggested Tom. (5) The jockey said, 'My job is riding horses.' (6) The cow said, 'Moo.' (7) 'Where is your book?' the tec asked. (8) 'It gets very hot in a bakery,' the baker said. (9) 'I can't do it!' Joanne exclaimed. (10) John screamed, 'Get away from me!'

Suffixes

Ready
read this

A suffix is a group of letters **that goes** at the end **of a word.**

Suffixes often change the meaning **of a word or the** job that the word does.

use + ful = useful

Steady
practise this

1 Complete these suffix sums.

use + less =

power + ful =

quick + ly =

mix + er =

pen + s =

cry + ing =

look + ed =

care + ful =

colour + less =

wise + ly =

2 Take off the suffix and write the word that you are left with.

painful pain

thoughtless

slowly

singer

rolled

helpless

printer

player

carrying

wonderful

You can do it!

ANSWERS: (1) useless, quickly, pens, looked, colourless, powerful, mixer, crying, careful, wisely; (2) pain; slow; roll; print; carry; thought; singer; help; play; wonder

Go test yourself

Choose a sensible suffix to complete each word.

1	colour	(ly/ful)
2	care	(less/ly)
3	bad	(ed/ly)
4	read	(ing/ed)
5	wash	(less/ed)
6	mix	(er/ful)
7	sharp	(ly/less)
8	end	(ful/less)
9	paint	(ing/ly)
10	brush	(ful/ed)

jump

ing

Colour a star ★ for each answer you get right.

How many different words can you make by adding different suffixes?

Suffix Box	ful	less	ing	ed	er	ly

Word Box

rough	power	plant	quiet	help	climb

ANSWERS: (1) colourful; (2) careless; (3) badly; (4) reading; (5) washed; (6) mixer; (7) sharply; 8) endless; (9) paint
(10) brushed

Pronouns

Ready read this

A pronoun is a word that takes the place of a noun.

Ben got muddy when he (Ben) fell in the puddle.

Here are the common pronouns:
I me we us you he him she her it they them

Steady practise this

1 Underline the pronoun in each sentence.

a The old lady sat down as she was tired.

b We are going to the park.

c Can you swim?

d The boy shouted when he saw the thief.

e The cat drank some milk when it came in.

f I love chips.

2 Write who or what each underlined pronoun stands for.

a Sam picked up the ball and threw it (the ball).

b Emma had a dog which she (__________) took everywhere.

c 'I (__________) like acting,' Tom said.

d 'Play with us (__________________),' Paul and Amy said.

e Jane wanted the dress but it (______) was too dear for her (______).

f 'Are you (__________) coming?' Mrs Allen asked Lara and John.

ANSWERS: 1 (a) she; (b) we; (c) you; (d) he; (e) it; (f) I
2 (a) the ball; (b) Emma; (c) Tom; (d) Paul and Amy; (e) the dress, Jane; (f) Lara and John

Go test yourself

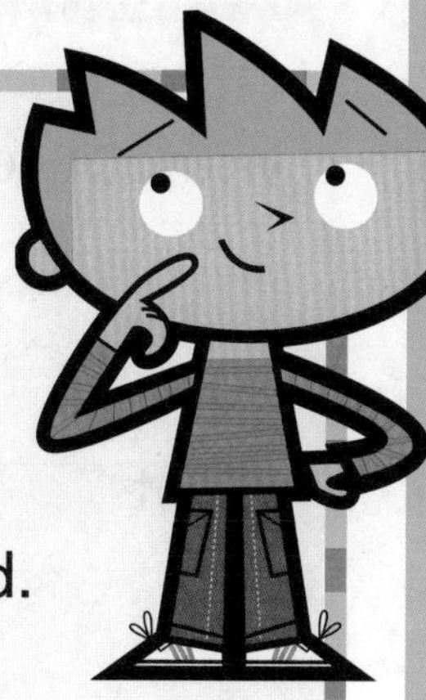

Choose the best pronoun to complete each sentence.

1 (I, You) ______ am very hungry.

2 The children laughed as (she, they) ______ played.

3 'Will (they, you) ______ please be quiet?' Mr Jones asked.

4 (They, It) ______ is very sunny today.

5 I called for Edward but (we, he) ______ was not in.

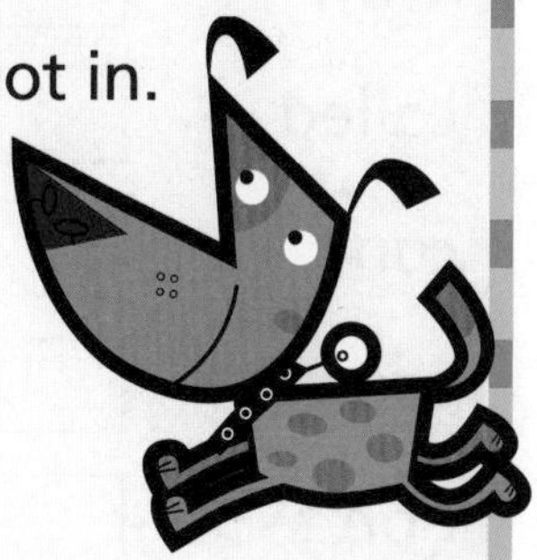

6 Are (it, you) ______ good at spelling?

7 My friend came to see ______ (I, me).

8 'Shall ______ (we, you) go out?' I asked the others.

9 Jack didn't like the weather because ______ (it, they) was cold.

10 'I saw ______ (you, us) in town yesterday,' Ben said to Cara.

Colour a star ★ for each answer you get right.

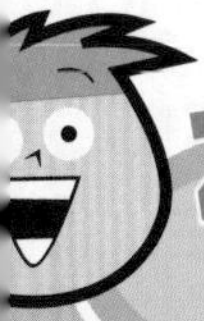

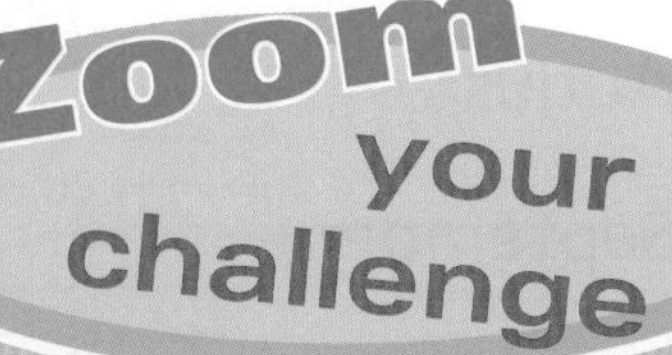

★ Take any page from a newspaper. How many of the pronouns in the box can you see? Circle any that you find.

I	me	we	us	you	he	him
she	he	it	they	them		

★ Which pronoun is used the most?

ANSWERS: (1) I; (2) they; (3) you; (4) It; (5) he; (6) you; (7) me; (8) we; (9) it; (10) you

Spell check

Check how many of these words you can read and spell without copying.

	Read correctly	Spell correctly		Read correctly	Spell correctly		Read correctly	Spell correctly
about			orange			Sunday		
after			people			Monday		
another			purple			Tuesday		
because			push			Wednesday		
blue			pull			Thursday		
called			school			Friday		
can't			should			Saturday		
could			sister			January		
don't			some			February		
father			their			March		
first			there			April		
half			they're			May		
last			these			June		
laugh			took			July		
love			wanted			August		
many			water			September		
mother			would			October		
next			your			November		
night			you're			December		
once			you've					